Gun Education and Safety

GUN SAFETY

BRIAN KEVIN

ABDO Publishing Company

visit us at
www.abdopublishing.com

Published by ABDO Publishing Company, PO Box 398166, Minneapolis, MN 55439.
Copyright © 2012 by Abdo Consulting Group, Inc. International copyrights reserved in all countries.
No part of this book may be reproduced in any form without written permission from the publisher.
The Checkerboard Library™ is a trademark and logo of ABDO Publishing Company.

Printed in the United States of America, North Mankato, Minnesota.
112011
012012

Cover Photo: AP Images
Interior Photos: Alamy pp. 21, 26; AP Images p. 13; Corbis p. 25; iStockphoto pp. 8–9, 22, 23, 28, 29;
    Megan M. Gunderson pp. 16, 17, 18, 19; Photo Researchers p. 7; Thinkstock pp. 5, 10–11, 14–15,
    15, 20, 24–25, 26–27

Extra special thanks to Autumn Freng.

Series Coordinator: Megan M. Gunderson
Editors: Megan M. Gunderson, BreAnn Rumsch
Art Direction: Neil Klinepier

Library of Congress Cataloging-in-Publication Data

Kevin, Brian, 1980-
  Gun safety / Brian Kevin.
     p. cm. -- (Gun education and safety)
  Includes index.
  ISBN 978-1-61783-316-8
  1. Firearms--Safety measures--Juvenile literature. 2. Firearms ownership--Juvenile literature. I.
Title.
  TS534.5.K48 2012
  683.4--dc23
                                    2011031414

CONTENTS

A Close Call

Elsa loved hunting with her dad. He had been hunting turkey in the woods behind their house since before Elsa was born. When she was 11, Elsa and her dad went to hunter safety class together. Last year, he was proud when she shot her first turkey.

But Elsa wasn't used to hunting with Uncle Rick. This was his first time hunting with Elsa and her dad. Uncle Rick liked to tell loud stories as they walked through the woods. Sometimes he waved his shotgun in the air while he talked. Elsa's dad had to remind him to carry it safely. "Hold it across your chest with two hands," he said. But Uncle Rick didn't listen.

On the way home, Elsa's uncle was telling another story. He was shaking his gun in the air with one hand. Suddenly, there was a loud pop. Elsa jumped while her dad and Uncle Rick ducked. Uncle Rick had accidentally fired his shotgun!

Everyone was fine, but Elsa's dad was very angry. Uncle Rick broke several important safety rules that day. He didn't carry his gun properly. He left it loaded when he didn't intend to fire it. And he left the safety switch turned off.

In the case of Elsa and her family, no one was hurt. But firearms can cause injury or even death. So, every gun user must know the rules and put safety first.

Safe hunters require everyone in their group to follow the rules.

Golden Rules

Different kinds of guns should be handled in different ways. And, some gun sports have their own special safety rules. Different states also enforce different sets of gun laws.

The specifics of gun safety can seem like a lot to keep track of. But there are golden rules that apply to all guns, in all places, no matter what.

Remember to treat every firearm as if it were loaded. Even parents and instructors can be wrong about unloaded weapons. So to be safe, always assume that a gun is loaded and ready to fire.

Your gun should only be loaded when you intend to fire it. So, wait to load your gun until you are ready to use it. Have you finished target practice? Are you heading back to the car after a long day of hunting? If you are done shooting, be sure you have unloaded your firearm.

Firearms should only be loaded when you're ready to use them.

When handling a gun, always keep it pointed in a safe direction. That means knowing where the **muzzle** is pointed at all times. Keep it pointed away from other people in case the gun fires unexpectedly. Never aim at anything you don't intend to shoot. This is true even if you think your gun is unloaded!

Always keep your finger off the **trigger** until you are ready to shoot. The trigger is not a place to rest your finger. You could trip or be startled and squeeze it accidentally. Almost all guns have a trigger guard that surrounds the trigger. Fingers belong outside the trigger guard unless you're about to shoot.

Before shooting, identify your target. Maybe you are hunting with a shotgun or a rifle. Or maybe you are shooting at a paper target with a pistol. Either way, never fire unless you're absolutely sure of your target. Don't simply shoot at sounds, movement, or patches of color. That brown shape in the bushes may not be the deer you're after!

Bullets travel fast and far. Be sure you know where your shot will go if you miss your target.

Permits and Registration

Even with the golden rules, guns can be dangerous in the wrong hands. So in the United States, the national and state governments regulate gun ownership. Gun laws are slightly different in each state. But, all gun owners must know them. Ignoring gun laws can lead to fines or even jail time.

Many states require permits to buy handguns, such as pistols or revolvers. Yet most states do not require permits to buy long guns. Hawaii is one state that does require permits to purchase shotguns and rifles. Massachusetts and Illinois require buyers to have special identification cards to make gun purchases.

Sometimes, buyers have to wait several days to take their guns home. Plus, those who wish to buy a gun must agree to a background check.

Certain individuals are not allowed to buy firearms. These include some convicted criminals and people suffering from mental illness.

Depending on where you live, certain types of guns may need to be registered with local police. Every gun has a **unique** serial number. Police record this number, along with the owner's name. That way, a gun can be returned if it is lost or stolen.

While some states don't require permits to buy guns, many require them to carry guns around.

Hunter Education

Most firearms used for hunting are rifles and shotguns. Special classes teach hunters how to use these weapons safely. These classes are called "hunter education" or "hunter safety."

Every US state and 10 Canadian provinces require hunters in certain age groups to pass hunter education. It is required to get a license.

The first hunter education classes started in the 1940s. After that, people realized that states requiring hunter education had fewer accidents. So today, more than 700,000 hunters are trained every year in hunter education programs throughout North America.

Hunter education classes teach more than the golden rules. They also teach hunters how to operate their firearms. Rifles and shotguns operate differently depending on the type of action they have. The action is all the parts that load, unload, fire, and **eject** the **ammunition**. The five types of actions are bolt, pump, lever, break, and semiautomatic.

In hunter education, safety always comes first.

Every action should have a safety switch. When the safety is on, the **trigger** cannot be pulled. That way, the gun can't fire by accident. But safety switches can fail. So always follow the golden rules, even when the safety is on!

Hunter education also teaches people how to use the right **ammunition** for their firearms. Hunters learn that the diameter of the inside of a rifle barrel is a measurement called caliber. For a shotgun barrel, this measurement is called gauge. These tell hunters which ammunition to use in their guns. Using the wrong size can cause serious injury.

Hunting safely isn't just about shooting **accurately**. It also is about knowing when not to fire. You should never shoot at unidentified animals. And when hunting with others, you should always know your safe zone of fire. That way, two hunters never fire at the same target.

Finally, hunter education classes teach more than just safety. New hunters learn about the sport's history and

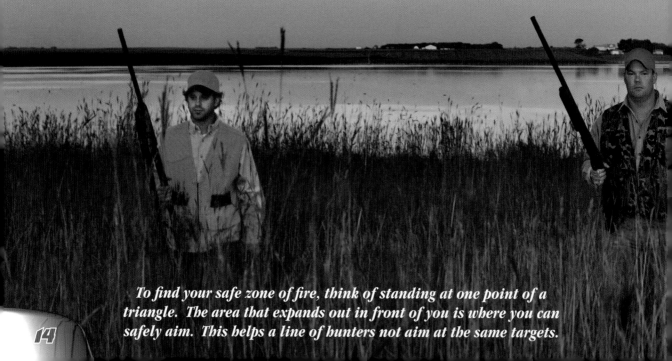

To find your safe zone of fire, think of standing at one point of a triangle. The area that expands out in front of you is where you can safely aim. This helps a line of hunters not aim at the same targets.

tradition. Students also learn to be respectful of wildlife and landowners. This is called a hunter's ethics. Respecting safety and ethics helps improve the sport's reputation.

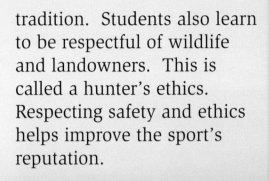

Caliber is used to describe the distance across the bore of a rifle or a handgun. The bore is the inside of the barrel. Gauge (GAYJ) describes the distance across a shotgun's bore. These distances are measured in millimeters or in decimals of an inch.

Caliber and gauge also refer to the size of ammunition. The correct sizes must be used! For example, a 16-gauge shotgun requires 16-gauge shells.

Caliber and gauge are marked on guns and ammunition. So, you'll always know what is safest to use.

Safe Carrying

After completing safety classes, you will be ready to go hunting. Whether taking aim at pheasants or heading to a deer stand, you will need to know how to safely carry your shotgun or rifle. There are many ways to do this.

The safest is the two-handed or "ready" carry. When using this carry, your firearm lays across your body with its **muzzle** up. One hand should cover the **trigger** guard. But remember, keep your fingers off the trigger! If someone is walking next to you, make sure the muzzle is not pointing in his or her direction.

Two-handed or "ready" carry

When facing someone, either the cradle carry or the shoulder carry might be a better option. The cradle carry points the gun's **muzzle** to the side. The gun's barrel rests in the crook of your elbow. Your hand holds the **stock**.

Using the shoulder carry, the gun's barrel rests on your shoulder. One hand holds the stock. This carry keeps the gun's muzzle pointing up and back. So, it should not be used if anyone is behind you.

Cradle carry

Shoulder carry

Elbow carry

Trail carry

If people are behind you or to your side, use the elbow carry or the trail carry. For the elbow carry, the gun rests on your forearm. The **stock** is tucked under your armpit. This carry is the least secure. So be sure you are not walking through high brush that could catch on the barrel.

Sling carry

For the trail carry, hold on to the gun's **stock** firmly with one hand. The **muzzle** will point forward and down, so be sure no one is in front of you. This carry also is not secure if you trip, so be aware of your path.

Your gun may have a sling. If so, it can hang on your shoulder. Just keep your thumb hooked in the sling. The muzzle should be behind you, pointed up. The sling carry is useful when you need your hands free. But it can be dangerous when walking through heavy brush.

Be sure to choose the carry that is safest for your situation and surroundings. And always remember the golden rules. Following these practices will help keep everyone safe while on the hunt.

Safety classes are also available for handgun owners. Some states even require these classes, especially for people who want to carry a weapon in public.

Many classes are offered by organizations such as the National Rifle Association (NRA). These courses teach students how to safely load and unload their guns. And, they often require a demonstration of **marksmanship**.

Remember, a pistol's chamber might hold a round even though the magazine has been removed.

Many modern pistols are semiautomatic. This means a **cartridge** is loaded automatically after each shot. But, the **trigger** must be pulled to shoot each time.

Small metal boxes called magazines hold cartridges, or **rounds** of **ammunition**. The

When loading or unloading a handgun, always keep your finger off the trigger.

magazine may be a part of the gun. Or, it may be a removable piece.

As with rifles, pistol barrels and cartridges have specific calibers. Not every cartridge that fits in a gun's magazine is safe to use. Only use those that match your pistol's caliber. Never shoot ammunition that is dirty, old, or wet. This can cause a gun to misfire or explode.

Handgun safety instructors also teach how to load and unload revolvers. In a revolver, cartridges are loaded into a rotating cylinder. The cylinder has **chambers** that fit one cartridge each. Unloading requires a small rod to push cartridges out.

Marksmanship

You don't need to own a gun to learn to shoot safely. Some ranges offer gun rentals and safety classes.

Many communities have shooting ranges. There, gun owners practice **marksmanship**. They may also participate in gun sports, such as clay shooting. At the range, expect to see rules posted about safe behavior and required safety equipment. Safety glasses and earplugs or earmuffs help protect your eyes and ears.

Shooting at indoor or outdoor targets can help improve **accuracy**. This is important for self-defense as well as for responsible hunters. A good shot won't endanger other hunters in the field. It also fulfills a responsibility to the animal. Accurate shooting guarantees a quick kill, so the animal doesn't suffer.

Many shooting ranges participate in the Civilian **Marksmanship** Program. This government program was created in 1903. Its original goal was to train citizens in case of war. Today, the program focuses on training and safety for youth.

FAIR CHASE

Responsible hunters do more than learn how to safely and accurately use their firearms. They obey all laws for what and where they are hunting. And, they hunt according to fair chase.

Fair chase means people do not hunt in ways that are unfair to their prey. For example, they hunt animals that are roaming freely but not those that are trapped. Respecting wildlife and acting in a sportsmanlike manner helps the reputation of all hunters.

Cases and Cars

You know safety is important at shooting ranges and on hunting grounds. But have you thought about safety when you're traveling to and from these places?

Always carry your firearm in a case. Some cases are soft, light, and padded. Others are hard and can be locked. If you're traveling by boat, waterproof cases are best.

In the United States, people are allowed to transport guns by car for all lawful purposes. However, important safety rules must be followed. A gun should always be unloaded. It should always be transported in a case. Even in a case, the **muzzle** should point away from people. And, the case should be locked in a trunk or other area passengers can't access.

To reach hunting grounds more easily, many hunters travel on all-terrain

A soft gun case

vehicles (ATVs). Riding ATVs can be fun, but they are not toys. As with cars and trucks, guns on ATVs should always be unloaded and in cases.

Be sure to wear a helmet when riding an ATV. This is just as important as how you carry your gun!

Guns at Home

Unfortunately, gun-related accidents do happen. And most of these accidents happen at home. A gun isn't safe just because it's tucked away in a closet or a drawer.

At home, gun owners should always store firearms in a locked safe or cabinet. In addition, guns should be kept separate from **ammunition**.

Locks are an easy, inexpensive way to help make gun storage safer.

The key for a trigger or cable lock should be kept separate from the gun.

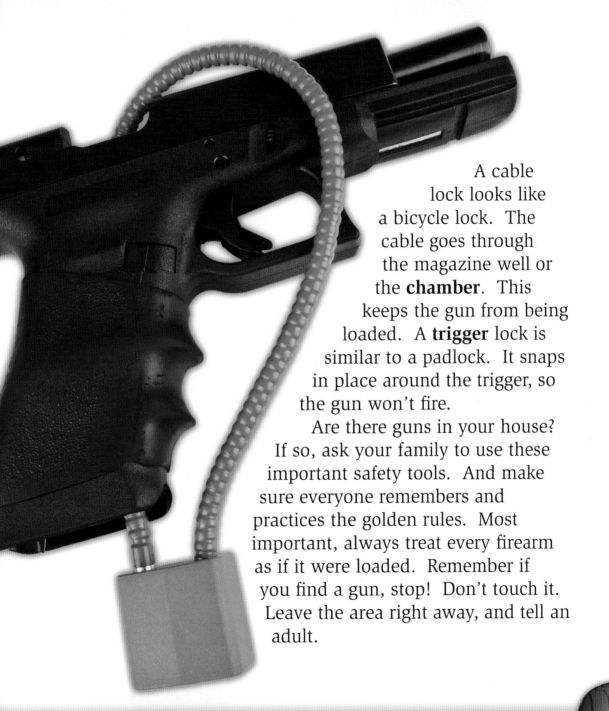

A cable
lock looks like
a bicycle lock. The
cable goes through
the magazine well or
the **chamber**. This
keeps the gun from being
loaded. A **trigger** lock is
similar to a padlock. It snaps
in place around the trigger, so
the gun won't fire.

Are there guns in your house?
If so, ask your family to use these
important safety tools. And make
sure everyone remembers and
practices the golden rules. Most
important, always treat every firearm
as if it were loaded. Remember if
you find a gun, stop! Don't touch it.
Leave the area right away, and tell an
adult.

Guns at School

Guns should never, ever be brought to a school. This rule applies to adults as well as kids. Only a few people, such as police officers, are allowed to carry guns in a school zone.

If you see someone with a gun at school, get away quickly and quietly. As soon as possible, talk to an adult you trust. Tell a teacher, principal, or counselor everything you remember. Who had the gun? What did it look like? What were they doing with it?

Even if a classmate is just showing off, it's not safe. As you have learned, even a gun that has been unloaded may still have a **round** in the **chamber**. Your classmate may claim the gun isn't loaded. But you should still get away and tell an adult.

At school, at home, in the field, and at the range, gun safety always comes first. Firearms are always tools and never toys.

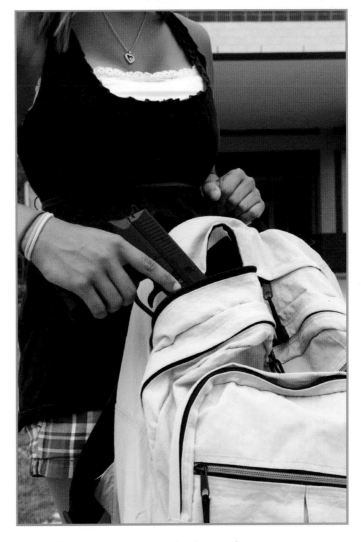

Responsible gun owners know how to properly buy, license, carry, and fire their guns. When guns are handled correctly, hunting and other shooting sports can be safe and fun!

If you see a gun at school, tell a trusted adult right away. This will help keep everyone safe.

GLOSSARY

accurate - free of errors.

ammunition - bullets, shells, cartridges, or other items used in firearms.

cartridge - a tube containing the explosive charge and bullet or shot to be fired from a weapon.

chamber - the part of a gun that holds the charge.

eject - to remove from inside something.

marksmanship - the skill of shooting a target.

muzzle - the open front end of the barrel of a weapon.

round - a bullet, shell, or cartridge used for a single shot.

stock - the usually wooden end of a firearm held against the shoulder for firing.

trigger - the small lever pulled back by the finger to fire a gun.

unique - being the only one of its kind.

WEB SITES

To learn more about gun safety, visit ABDO Publishing Company online. Web sites about gun safety are featured on our Book Links page. These links are routinely monitored and updated to provide the most current information available.

www.abdopublishing.com

INDEX

32741